ROD SERLING's THE TWILIGHT ZONE

DEATHS-HEAD REVISITED

Adaptation from Rod Serling's original script by

MARK KNEECE

Illustrated by

CHRIS LIE

WITHDRAWN FROM STOCK

OMSBURY

ERLIN NEW YORK

INTRODUCTION

There is a fifth dimension beyond that which is known to man. It is a dimension as vast as space and timeless as infinity. It is the middle ground between light and shadow, between science and superstition, and it lies between the pit of man's fears and the summit of his knowledge. This is the dimension of imagination. It is an area which we call the Twilight Zone.

America, between the 1950s and early 1960s, was itself in a sort of "twilight zone." Following the victories of World War II and the attending economic boom—but before the Civil Rights marches; the assassinations of John F. Kennedy, Martin Luther King, Jr., and Robert F. Kennedy; and the Vietnam War—we were wrapped in a gleaming package of shining chrome, white picket fences, and Hollywood glamour. But beneath this shimmering facade lay a turbulent core of racial inequality, sexual inequality, and the Cold War threat of nuclear attacks from the Soviet Union. We'd never been more affluent—or more frightened.

Enter Rodman Edward Serling of Binghamton, New York. Serling began writing in his teens for his high school newspaper; as a student at Antioch College, he was already selling scripts to radio programs. While serving as a paratrooper in the U.S. Army Eleventh Airborne (for which he earned a Purple Heart), he wrote for the Armed Services Radio. He went on to write for film and television, first in feature presentations for *Hallmark Hall of Fame* and *Playhouse 90*, including the lauded "Requiem for a Heavyweight," perhaps drawing inspiration from his own experiences as a Golden Gloves boxer. More than two hundred of his teleplays were produced. In all, his work would win not only the adoration of listeners and viewers but a host of prestigious awards, including a record-breaking six Emmy awards—two of them for his greatest achievement, *The Twilight Zone*.

The worlds and characters presented over the course of five seasons, beginning in October 1959, were like nothing audiences had seen before. Television, the new "must have" appliance for America's increasingly prosperous households, offered comedies such as *I Love Lucy* and *The Honeymooners*, news programs including Edward R. Murrow's *See It Now*, as well as Westerns, game shows, and soap operas. With a typewriter as his spade, Serling dug beneath the surface of the expected and planted the seeds of a more imaginative and thoughtful genre, writing more than half of the show's 156 episodes while producing and hosting all of them. He bravely took on themes of oppression, prejudice, and paranoia, all the while giving people what they needed at the end of the day: entertainment.

While he had his run-ins with censorship, Serling's clever use of other worlds and veiled scenarios generally protected him. As he explained, what he couldn't have a Republican or a Democrat espouse on the show, he could have an alien profess without offending the sponsors. This approach also allowed viewers to take away whatever message best suited them; the more reflective could consider the psychological and political implications, while others might be satisfied with simply enjoying the thrill of the surface story. So much more than mere science fiction or fantasy, Serling's scripts are parables that explore the multifaceted natures of hope, fear, humanity, loneliness, and self-delusion.

Half a century later, *The Twilight Zone* remains a part of our culture, routinely referenced in print and on television, having become a shorthand expression that succinctly describes the bizarre and unexpected. The original episodes are still aired on the SciFi Channel, both in late-night slots and as day-long marathons. The show was literally a Who's Who of Hollywood, helping to foster the careers of fledgling actors including Robert Redford, Ron Howard, Dennis Hopper, Charles Bronson, and William Shatner. It has also inspired countless authors and filmmakers, who have gone on to break through boundaries of their own.

In the fifty years since *The Twilight Zone* first aired, we've faced new enemies and have altered our definitions of happiness, but our core hopes and fears remain the same, as does our desire to be entertained. The stories are as compelling, and as telling, as ever. And now, in their newest incarnation, Serling's scripts serve as the basis for this graphic novel series, which honors the original text and even echoes the storyboarding of television, but offers a fresh interpretation, as seen through the eyes of a new generation of artists.

—Anna Marlis Burgard
Director of Industry Partnerships, Savannah College of Art and Design

You're traveling through
another dimension,
a dimension not only of sight and sound
but of mind;
a journey into a wondrous land
whose boundaries
are that of imagination.
That's the signpost up ahead—
your next stop,
the Twilight Zone!

I WAS ONLY FOLLOWING MY ORDERS.

I ONLY DID WHAT I HAD TO DO.

WHAT I HAD TO . . .

PLEASE! NO!

LET ME GET YOU SOME HELP.

LET HIM GO. HE'S BEEN THROUGH ENOUGH.

SIXTY-FOUR YEARS LATER...

Jingle
Jingle

WELCOME

YES?

YOU HAVE ACCOMMODATIONS HERE?

I CAN GIVE YOU A LOVELY FRONT ROOM OVERLOOKING THE SQUARE. WOULD YOU CARE TO SEE IT?

I'M SURE IT WILL BE SATISFACTORY.

THERE WAS SOMETHING?

I'M SORRY, NO. I-I ONLY NEED TO FIND YOUR KEY.

MR. . . . SCHMIDT?

THAT'S WHAT I'VE WRITTEN.

OF COURSE, SIR.

I JUST WONDERED . . .

YOU JUST WONDERED *WHAT*?

YOU REMIND ME OF SOMEONE, MR. SCHMIDT.

OH?

. . . THERE
WERE . . .

. . . SS
STATIONED
HERE DURING
THE WAR.

THEY OFTEN
USED TO COME
TO THE INN
WHEN THEY WERE
OFF DUTY.

EVERYTHING
OKAY?

I BELIEVE
I'LL TAKE A WALK
AROUND TOWN.

YOU'LL BE HERE LONG?

I DON'T REALLY KNOW. NOT LONG.

VERY QUAINT, THIS VILLAGE. PICTURESQUE.

AND YOU'VE NOT BEEN HERE BEFORE?

CERTAINLY NOT.

BUT I'M TOLD THE SCENERY IS LOVELY...

...THAT THERE IS A MEDIEVAL CASTLE ONE CAN VISIT.

THERE'S VERY LITTLE ELSE OF PARTICULAR INTEREST.

WASN'T THERE A PRISON OR SOMETHING HERE?

THERE WAS A CAMP.

HOW'S THAT?

A CAMP, HERR SCHMIDT. DURING THE WAR.

...TURNED INTO A SHRINE?

YOU SEEM FAMILIAR...

I FEEL THAT...

...SOMEHOW...

jingle jingle

...I KNOW YOU.

MR. SCHMIDT, A ROBUST EIGHTY-FIVE-YEAR-OLD MAN, IN GOOD HEALTH, POSSESSING A SHARP, VIGOROUS MIND . . .

. . . HAS JUST CHECKED INTO A ROOM IN DACHAU, A PICTURESQUE, DELIGHTFUL LITTLE SPOT ONCE KNOWN FOR ITS SCENERY . . .

. . . BUT NOW KNOWN FOR OTHER EVENTS HAVING TO DO WITH SOME OF THE LESS POSITIVE PURSUITS OF MAN . . .

. . . HUMAN SLAUGHTER, TORTURE, MISERY, AND ANGUISH.

MR. SCHMIDT HAS A VESTED INTEREST IN THE RUINS OF A CONCENTRATION CAMP.

SOME SIXTY YEARS AGO, HIS NAME WAS GUNTHER LUTZE. CAPTAIN IN THE SS. A UNIFORMED, STRUTTING ANIMAL, WHOSE FUNCTION IN LIFE WAS TO GIVE PAIN.

AND LIKE HIS COLLEAGUES OF THE TIME, HE SHARES THE ONE AFFLICTION MOST COMMON AMONGST THAT BREED KNOWN AS NAZIS...

...HE WALKS THE EARTH WITHOUT A HEART.

AND NOW FORMER SS CAPTAIN GUNTHER LUTZE WILL REVISIT HIS OLD HAUNTS...

...SATISFIED PERHAPS THAT ALL THAT IS AWAITING HIM IS AN ELEMENT OF NOSTALGIA.

ARBEIT MACHT FREI

WHAT HE DOES NOT KNOW, OF COURSE, IS THAT A PLACE LIKE DACHAU CANNOT EXIST ONLY IN BAVARIA.

BY ITS NATURE . . . BY ITS VERY NATURE . . . IT MUST BE ONE OF THE POPULATED AREAS OF . . . THE TWILIGHT ZONE.

GOOD AFTERNOON! HOW ARE YOU?

THE MEMORIAL WILL CLOSE SOON.

THE IMPORTANT SITES HAVE PLAQUES. THERE ARE MANY PICTURES TOO.

JA! THE MEMORIAL IS OPEN FROM 9 A.M. TO 5 P.M. THAT DOESN'T GIVE YOU VERY MUCH—

NINE TO FIVE?

THERE IS A MAP IN THE BROCHURE IF YOU—

WE WILL BE CLOSING SOON.

ALL RIGHT, PIGS—UP. TIME TO GREET THE MORNING. **ON YOUR FEET, FILTH!**

WE HAVE A NICE DAY AHEAD OF US. THE TEMPERATURE'S JUST SLIGHTLY BELOW ZERO.

WE WILL DO SOME EXERCISES. I AND YOU. I AND YOU. **I AND YOU.**

YOU WILL ASSEMBLE IN THE SQUARE, UNDRESSED.

IF SOME FILTH GETS CRUSHED BENEATH OUR BOOTS, SO BE IT. IT IS BEST!

TOGETHER WE BUILD THE FATHERLAND!

SIGH

YES, WE DID IMPRESSIVE WORK ONCE, DIDN'T WE?

AND NOW IT IS CLOSING TIME AT FIVE...

...AND WALKING MAPS.

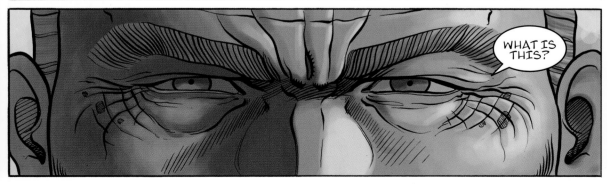

WHAT IS THIS?

WELCOME BACK, CAPTAIN.

YOU ARE SOME HIRED ACTOR, PERHAPS? HERE TO MAKE THE CAMP SEEM MORE REALISTIC?

I AM SORRY, IT IS CLOSING TIME.

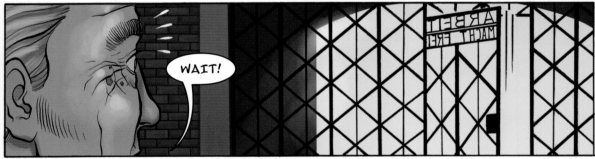

WAIT!

IT IS NOT TIME!

YOU CANNOT CLOSE!

I AM STILL IN HERE! DO YOU HEAR ME?

YES, IT IS BECKER. I KNOW YOU NOW!

HOW KIND. THE CAPTAIN REMEMBERS ME.

REMEMBER YOU? MY PRIZE PUPIL... ISN'T THAT WHAT I USED TO CALL YOU?

YOU—YOU DON'T SEEM TO HAVE CHANGED AT ALL.

THAT'S IT! IT'S BEEN SIXTY YEARS OR MORE! YOU HAVEN'T CHANGED.

SIXTY-FOUR YEARS, CAPTAIN LUTZE.

ARE YOU THE CARETAKER AROUND HERE?

IN A MANNER OF SPEAKING.

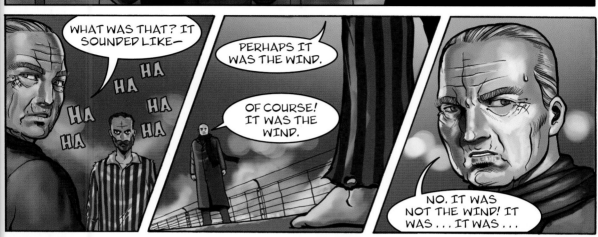

ODD THAT IT SHOULD DISTURB YOU. IT NEVER USED TO BOTHER YOU . . .

. . . WHEN YOUR VICTIMS SCREAMED!

BUT NOW THEY ARE NOT SCREAMING. THEY ARE SIMPLY REACTING.

AAAAAAH HA HA HA HA AAAAAAAEEEEiii !

THEY HAVE HEARD YOU OFFER THE EXCUSE USED BY ALL THE MONSTERS OF OUR TIME.

"WE DID AS WE WERE TOLD."

"WE FUNCTIONED AS ORDERED."

"WE MERELY OBEYED DIRECTIVES FROM SUPERIORS."

IT WAS THE THEME MUSIC AT NUREMBERG.

THE PLAINTIVE LITANY OF THE MASTER RACE AS IT LAY DYING.

TEN MILLION HUMAN BEINGS WERE KILLED— IN CAMPS LIKE THIS!

WOMEN, CHILDREN, TIRED OLD MEN . . .

YOU CHANGED YOUR NAME.

YOU WERE QUITE SAFE DOWN THERE IN SOUTH AMERICA.

WHAT COULD POSSIBLY HAVE BROUGHT YOU BACK HERE?

ONE MISSES THE FATHERLAND, HIS HOMELAND, BECKER.

ONE GROWS NOSTALGIC FOR THE GOOD OLD DAYS.

I HAD **HOPED** THAT WITH THE PASSAGE OF TIME . . . SANITY WOULD HAVE RETURNED.

I HAD HOPED THAT PEOPLE WOULD NOT SUCCUMB TO THE ANIMAL SCREAMS FOR VENGEANCE.

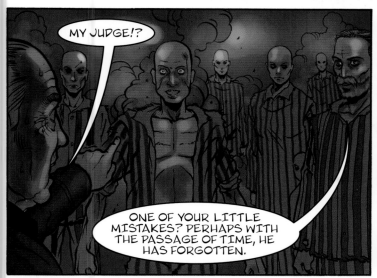

MY JUDGE!?

ONE OF YOUR LITTLE MISTAKES? PERHAPS WITH THE PASSAGE OF TIME, HE HAS FORGOTTEN.

WHAT IS THIS NONSENSE?

WHO ARE THESE FIENDS?

I AM YOUR PROSECUTOR.

PROSECUTOR? HA!

THE TRIAL HAS BEGUN. THE TESTIMONY IS UNDER WAY, CAPTAIN LUTZE. SHALL I READ THE INDICTMENTS AGAINST YOU?

YOU CAN KINDLY LET ME OUT OF HERE!

INDICTMENT ONE: THAT HE CONDEMNED TO DEATH WITHOUT A TRIAL ELEVEN HUNDRED HUMAN BEINGS GUILTY OF NOTHING.

THE INMATES OF COMPOUND SIX, DACHAU CONCENTRATION CAMP, VERSUS GUNTHER LUTZE, CAPTAIN, SS . . .

INDICTMENT TWO: THAT HE DID MAIM AND TORTURE WITHOUT PROVOCATION—THAT HE TOOK PLEASURE IN SAID TORTURE.

INDICTMENT THREE: THAT HE EXISTS EVEN NOW WITHOUT CONSCIENCE, WITHOUT REMORSE, WITHOUT A SINGLE FEELING OF KINDNESS FOR HIS FELLOW HUMAN BEINGS.

YOU'RE INSANE, BECKER!

INDICTMENT FOUR: THAT CAPTAIN LUTZE SHOT DOWN INNOCENT CHILDREN, WOMEN, AND MEN SIMPLY TO PREVENT THEM FROM REVEALING HIS CRIMES.

THAT CAPTAIN LUTZE COMMITTED THESE ATROCITIES . . .

. . . AT THE VERY MOMENT . . .

. . . WHEN SAID CHILDREN, WOMEN, AND MEN . . .

. . . WERE BEGINNING TO HAVE SOME HOPE . . .

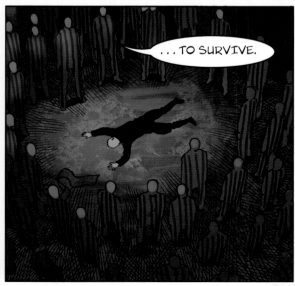

. . . TO SURVIVE.

UNN . . .

Dong!

Kerrrretch

YOU HAVE BEEN UNCONSCIOUS FOR A WHILE.

BECKER!

I FELL ASLEEP.

I HAD SUCH A DREAM.

YOU HAD NO DREAM, CAPTAIN.

OF COURSE I HAD A DREAM.

THERE WERE PEOPLE, MANY PEOPLE.

SOME OF THEM CRAWLED OUT OF THE OVENS—IT WAS HORRIBLE TO BEHOLD.

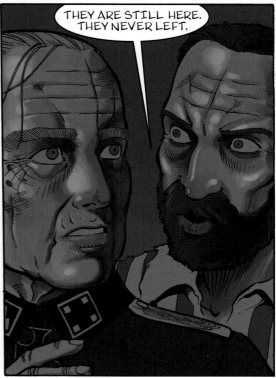

THEY ARE STILL HERE. THEY NEVER LEFT.

THE TRIAL . . . ?

THE TRIAL IS OVER. YOU HAVE BEEN FOUND GUILTY. IT'S TIME TO PRONOUNCE SENTENCE.

YOU ARE GOING TO . . . TO . . .

YOU ARE GOING TO PRONOUNCE SENTENCE? THIS IS WHAT YOU HAVE IN MIND NOW?

YOU WILL—WILL— PRONOUNCE **MY** SENTENCE. AND THEN YOU—YOU! AH HA HA HA!

AND THEN YOU SHALL EXECUTE THAT SENTENCE? IS THIS—IS THIS CORRECT? HEH HEH . . .

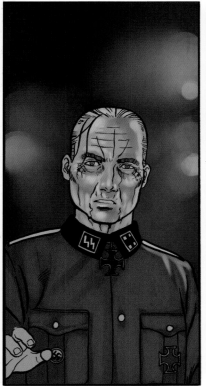

PIGS! FILTH!

YOU WILL ALL ASSEMBLE IN THE SQUARE. HA HA! YOU WILL PASS SENTENCE ON CAPTAIN LUTZE!

THEN YOU WILL ALL KINDLY CRAWL BACK INTO THE OVEN! HA HA!

WHERE ARE THEY? WHERE IS THE JUDGE? WHERE IS THE JURY? WHERE IS THE EXECUTIONER?

SHALL I TELL YOU WHERE THEY ARE, BECKER?

THEY'RE IN YOUR MIND.

YOU HAVE HATCHED THEM OUT OF YOUR HATRED. YOU HAVE PLANNED YOUR VENGEANCE OUT OF A CRAZY QUILT OF IMAGINATION.

SEWN TOGETHER WITH LITTLE THIN THREADS OF WISHFUL THINKING.

WHY DIDN'T I KILL YOU WHEN I HAD THE CHANCE?

BECKER. BECKER, I DID KILL YOU. I KILLED YOU THE DAY . . .

AT THIS GATE, YOU SHOT DOWN HUNDREDS OF PEOPLE WITH MACHINE GUNS.

DO YOU FEEL THE BULLETS SMASHING INTO YOUR BODY?

DO YOU FEEL THE AGONY OF TEARING LEAD?

UHHN . . . HRT . . .

TAT TAT TAT TAT TAT TAT!

NO . . . NO . . . LEAVE ME ALONE . . .

ON THESE POSTS YOU STRUNG UP HUMAN BEINGS TO DIE.

HAVE MERCY.

DO YOU FEEL THEIR AGONY?

HUHN . . . HUHN . . .

GAH, NO! LEAVE ME ALONE! HUHN . . .

IN THIS ROOM, CAPTAIN— THE THINGS YOU DID TO HUMAN BEINGS ARE UNMENTIONABLE.

WATER... PLEASE...

THERE IS NO WATER FOR YOU, LUTZE.

NO WATER, NO REPRIEVE.

YEEEEEAAAAAHHH!!

AAAAAA . . .

AAAAA . . .
MMMMMMRRRNNNN . . .

CAPTAIN LUTZE . . .
IF YOU CAN STILL
REASON . . .

. . . IF THERE IS
ANY PORTION OF YOUR
MIND THAT CAN STILL
FUNCTION . . .

. . . TAKE THIS THOUGHT WITH
YOU. THIS IS NOT HATRED.

THIS IS
RETRIBUTION.
THIS IS NOT
REVENGE.

THIS IS JUSTICE.

YOUR *FINAL* JUDGMENT WILL COME FROM GOD.

IT APPEARS THAT I'LL HAVE TO GO IN AND GET HIM.

GOOD LORD!

MOMENTS LATER

HE WAS SCREAMING WHEN WE TRIED TO HELP HIM.

SUCH SCREAMS. LIKE AN ANIMAL.

THAT SHOULD DO IT.

HE IS SO FULL OF SEDATIVES NOW THAT HE DOESN'T KNOW HE IS ON EARTH.

I WANT HIM STRAPPED TO THE BED.

WHAT HAPPENED TO HIM? HE WASN'T IN THERE TWENTY MINUTES.

HE SCREAMS FROM PAIN. MORE THAN PAIN— AGONY.

HE HAD THIS IN HIS POCKET. SCHLAFEN GASTHOF, SEE?

MAYBE SOMEONE KNOWS ABOUT HIM, MIND IF I CHECK?

IF YOU LIKE.

LATER

HE SAID NOTHING TO YOU?

ONLY THAT HE WISHED TO VISIT DACHAU.

DACHAU! WHY DOES IT STILL STAND? WHY DO WE KEEP IT AS A MEMORIAL?

GOD KNOWS . . .

THERE IS AN ANSWER TO THE DOCTOR'S QUESTION.

ALL THE DACHAUS MUST REMAIN STANDING.

THE DACHAUS, THE BELSENS, THE BUCHENWALDS, THE AUSCHWITZES.

ALL OF THEM A MONUMENT TO A MOMENT IN TIME WHEN A FEW MEN DECIDED TO TURN THE EARTH INTO A GRAVEYARD.

INTO IT THEY SHOVELED ALL OF THEIR REASON, THEIR LOGIC, THEIR KNOWLEDGE, BUT WORST OF ALL, THEIR CONSCIENCE.

PAPA...

Deaths-Head Revisited

Season Three, Episode #9

Original Air Date: November 10, 1961

Written by Rod Serling

Cast

Narrator: Rod Serling

Becker: Joseph Schildkraut*
*Also appeared in *The Trade-Ins* as John Holt

SS Captain Gunther Lutze: Oscar Beregi Jr.*
*Also appeared in *Mute* as Professor Karl Werner
and *The Rip Van Winkle Caper* as Farwell the Ringleader

Innkeeper: Kaaren Verne (as Karen Verne)

Taxi Driver: Robert Boon (as Robert Boone)*
*Also appeared in *Mute* as Holger Nielsen

Doctor: Ben Wright*
*Also appeared in *Dead Man's Shoes* as Chips
and *Judgment Night* as Captain Wilbur

Dachau Victim: Chuck Fox

Crew

Producer: Buck Houghton
Director: Don Medford
Director of Photography: Jack Swain
Film Editor: Bill Mosher

Production Note

Deaths-Head Revisited was inspired by the trial of Nazi war criminal Adolf Eichmann, which began in April 1961 and ended with his conviction on December 11, 1961, almost exactly one month after this episode aired. Considered by many to be the architect of the Final Solution, Eichmann escaped after the war and was found in Argentina by Israeli agents, who abducted him and brought him to Israel, where he was tried, convicted, and executed. So, like Lutze, Eichmann was put on trial and brought to justice by Jewish victims of the Holocaust. In another parallel to the Holocaust, two years before he appeared in this episode as Becker, Joseph Schildkraut played Anne Frank's father in the movie *The Diary of Anne Frank.*

ADAPTING STORIES FROM ROD SERLING'S
THE TWILIGHT ZONE

In terms of screenwriting adaptations it's trying to cut out stuff that's extraneous, without doing damage to the original piece, because you owe a debt of some respect to the original author.

—Rod Serling, 1975

At first, the idea sounded straightforward. Take an original *Twilight Zone* screenplay and adapt it into a graphic novel—break the visuals into panels, move the dialogue into balloons and captions. After all, Rod Serling himself was a fan of comics, and graphic novels are their visual and literary heirs. Serling collected Entertaining Comics titles such as *Tales from the Crypt* and *Weird Science*, the themes of which resonate in *The Twilight Zone*; even Serling's trademark narration could be considered an echo of the Crypt Keeper's introductions. Yet the more I considered the task of adapting the scripts, the more the gravity of what I was doing set in. I grew up watching *The Twilight Zone*, after all, as did so many Americans. The work required a certain reverential perspective, considering the show's iconic status, not to mention the quality of the original material.

In the 1950s the comics Serling had enjoyed were considered subversive, a threat to America's youth. Frederick Wertham published *Seduction of the Innocent* in 1954, excoriating comics in an atmosphere of public paranoia similar to a scene from *The Monsters Are Due on Maple Street*. A year later, a Senate committee was convened to investigate the pernicious influence of horror comics on America's youth, and the Comics Code Authority was established to censor comics' content. EC Comics went out of business as a direct result. In an interesting twist of fate, by the end of the decade *The Twilight Zone* was just beginning to find its television audience with stories that probably would not have made it past the comics censors. Recreating Serling's stories now, in graphic novel form, seems appropriate, emblematic of an era in which comics are finding a new readership, achieving new respect, and speaking to a new audience receptive to a more sophisticated message.

Serling's stories run the gamut from serious drama, filled with fantastic and frightening dilemmas of the human condition, to wry, tongue-in-cheek humor in a sci-fi wrapper. Selecting eight as graphic novel material meant making difficult choices. Serling was a prolific writer, creating more than half of *The Twilight Zone*'s 156 scripts. It was not only a question of which of these would work best in novelized format, but which ones, as a group, would come closest to capturing the essence of *The Twilight Zone*. The stories ultimately chosen for these books possess the strongest visual possibilities and reflect an effort to achieve a cross section of Serling's dramatic range.

As I began adapting the stories for artists, I immersed myself in the screenplays and watched each episode until I felt I had internalized not just the characters, the plot, and the point, but what I imagined to be something of the author himself. In the process, I felt a growing kinship with Serling. Parts of the screenplay were often deleted from the actual show. Lines, characters, even entire scenes were struck, sometimes for budgetary reasons, sometimes because of time constraints, sometimes perhaps because Serling himself may have anticipated problems with the scenes. The show usually had only a thirty-minute time slot. The deleted scenes, however, often add richness and complexity to the story, offering a glimmer into what Serling might have done were it not for the constraints of the television medium. Restoring scenes seemed to help push the story even harder. I felt as if I were developing Serling's original design, following the telling to its logical conclusion.

With each of these stories, I have aspired to take advantage of what the graphic novel format can do. Art and text draw the reader deeply into the narrative. The reader does not just hear, but ponders, actively bridging the gaps between the panels of art with his or her own imagination. The story doesn't just happen to the reader, but, in part, *is* the reader. In other words, *The Twilight Zone* episodes had to be recreated not just to fit into a graphic novel format but to belong to it.

As much as possible, I have endeavored to keep the intentions of the original story intact—that is the "debt of respect" owed to Serling—fully functional in a new medium. From some nearby fifth dimension, I hope Serling is smiling at the prospect of these books, pleased at the thought of a new generation arriving by way of a different avenue perhaps, but entering and being welcomed into the fold of "Zonies" around the world.

—Mark Kneece
Professor of Sequential Art, Savannah College of Art and Design

Acknowledgments

Our thanks go to Carol Serling for her time and consideration while reviewing the adaptation
texts and illustrated pages, and also to John Lowe, chair of the Sequential Art Department at Savannah
College of Art and Design, for his assistance in pairing the right artists with the right stories.

Bloomsbury Publishing, London, Berlin and New York

First published in Great Britain in 2009 by Bloomsbury Publishing Plc
36 Soho Square, London, W1D 3QY

First published in the USA in 2009 by Walker & Company
175 Fifth Avenue, New York, NY 10010

Text copyright © 2008 by Savannah College of Art and Design, Inc.
Based on an original teleplay copyright © 1961 by The Rod Serling Trust, as assignee
Illustrations copyright © 2009 by Savannah College of Art and Design, Inc.
Introduction copyright © 2008 by Savannah College of Art and Design, Inc.
"Adapting Stories from Rod Serling's *The Twilight Zone*" copyright © 2008 by Savannah College of Art and Design, Inc.
The moral rights of the author and illustrator have been asserted

Packaged by Design Press, a division of Savannah College of Art and Design, Inc.®
22 East Lathrop Street, Savannah, Georgia 31415, USA

Adaptation from Rod Serling's original script by Mark Kneece
Illustrated by Chris Lie and Caravan Studio
Lettering by Thomas Zielonka
Series title treatment by Devin O'Bryan
Series copyediting by Kerri O'Hern
Series creative development by Anna Marlis Burgard and Emily Easton
Series art direction and design by Angela Rojas
Series project management by Angela Rojas and Melissa Kavonic
Creative consultant: Carol Serling

Photograph of Rod Serling © Bettmann/Corbis

A CIP catalogue record of this book is available from the British Library

ISBN 978 0 7475 8784 2

Printed in China by C & C Offset

1 3 5 7 9 10 8 6 4 2

All papers used by Bloomsbury Publishing are natural, recyclable products made from wood grown in well-managed forests.
The manufacturing processes conform to the environmental regulations of the country of origin

www.bloomsbury.com/childrens
The Savannah College of Art and Design: www.scad.edu